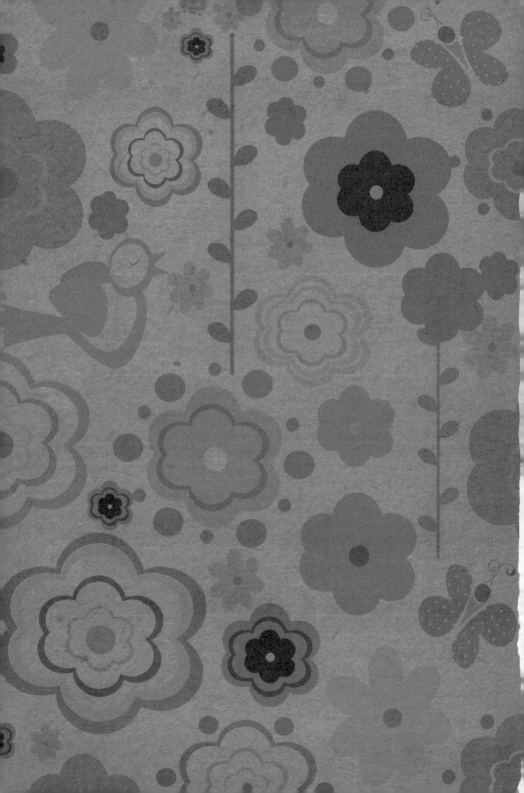

THE GIRL FILES

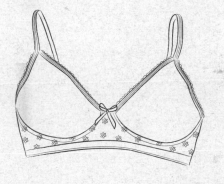

THE GIRL FILES

All about puberty & growing up....

JACQUI BAILEY

WAYLAND

First published in 2012 by Wayland

Copyright © Wayland 2012

Wayland
338 Euston Road
London NW1 3BH

Wayland Australia
Level 17/207 Kent Street
Sydney, NSW 2000

Editor: Debbie Foy
Design: Simon Daley, Giraffe

British Library Cataloguing in Publication Data
Bailey, Jacqui.
  The girl files : all about puberty and growing up.
  1. Puberty--Juvenile literature. 2. Adolescence--Juvenile
literature. 3. Girls--Life skills guides--Juvenile
literature.
  I. Title
  305.2'355-dc23

ISBN: 978 0 7502 7054 0

Printed in China

Wayland is a division of Hachette Children's Books,
an Hachette UK company

www.hachette.co.uk

CONTENTS

welcome to
the GIRL
FILES

 **Hi!** This book has been written totally and utterly for you! It's about your body and what happens when you start growing from a child into an adult. It's also about your *feelings* and the ways these can change, too. Like how you can suddenly start feeling really **NERVOUS** or **embarrassed** about things you hardly even noticed before. Or how one minute you're feeling *really happy,* and the next totally down in the dumps.

All this stuff happens because of something called puberty — and the good news is that you are not alone, because it happens to everybody! Yes, that's right, **EVERYBODY**. Even these people have gone through puberty:

☆ your mum

☆ the girl who lives next door

☆ your geography teacher

☆ your fave pop star

And what's more, everybody worries about whether the things that are happening are normal, or whether something **totally weird** is going on and they will turn into some kind of post-puberty **FREAK!** (Relax. It never happens.)

THE GIRL FILES has got all the stuff you need to know about how your body will change — and why — and the kinds of emotional *ups* and *downs* you might go through along the way. It's got loads of advice on stuff like friendships, bullying and boys, and lots of handy tips for dealing with all sorts of potentially **embarrassing** disasters. And best of all, it's there whenever you need it.

7

CHAPTER ONE

P IS FOR PUPPIES, PINK AND...
PUBERTY

Puberty can sometimes sound like some terrible sort of 'test' that you have to get through, but really it is the most natural thing in the world. It's just your body getting ready for the next stage in life.

☆✦⋅✦☆✦☆✦⋆✦☆✦☆✦⋆✦⋆✦☆✦

Puberty means that you're **growing up**. Your body is changing from a child's to an adult's. You get **taller** and your shape changes, you grow breasts, and you start having periods (more on that later). The reason for this is so that one day you will be able to have babies – if you want to.

Okay, so growing up can be a **SCARY** thought. The changes your body goes through are quite **amazing**, so it's no wonder we find the whole thing a bit worrying at times. But it is exciting too. Think of it as a whole new adventure.

CRAZY CHEMICALS

So who can you blame when your body starts doing **WEIRD** stuff? No, it's not your mum's fault or your dad's, or even the dog's. It's all down to things called hormones.

Hormones are **chemicals** that zip around in your bloodstream, carrying messages from one part of your body to another part. You have **thousands** of hormones in your body and they do all sorts of things, but mostly they work like tiny controllers – telling bits of your body when to start doing something or when to stop.

Hormones tell your body when you need to sleep or to wake up, when you need to eat or when you don't, when to warm up or when to cool down. They can make you feel **energetic and full of beans**, or washed out and grumpy. They also tell your body when to start puberty.

One day, in the middle of all the usual stuff – maths homework, watching telly, taking the dog for a walk, arguing with your big brother – your brain does something completely sneaky and entirely without asking you. It sends out a message telling other bits of your body to begin making sex hormones. And before you know it, your body starts changing.

FACT OR MYTH?

'Everyone's started puberty by the time they're 13.'

MYTH!

There's no exact age when you start puberty. It can happen at any time from the age of about 8 up to 16. However, it quite often starts between about 10 and 13 – or at least it does for girls.

Boys go through puberty as well, and their changes are just as powerful and as complicated as yours – even if they are a bit different. But girls usually start puberty a year or so before boys. Which puts us one step ahead – as usual, eh girls?

The thing is not to get too hung up about when you will start. Puberty takes time and your body will get going when it is ready and not before. You could be the first person in your class or or you could be the last. And while that might make you feel a bit awkward, how you feel makes no difference at all to your body.

CHECK IT OUT!

For all you list lovers, here are the main changes that happen to your body during puberty. Looks like a pretty long list, huh? But before you dive under your duvet and refuse to come out, it's not as bad as it looks.

They don't all happen at the same time, or in this order. And most of them happen slowly so you may not even notice for a while. In fact, the whole thing usually takes at least a few years from start to finish.

- ❀ You have a 'growth spurt' and get taller.
- ❀ Your hands and feet get bigger.
- ❀ Your arms and legs get longer.
- ❀ Your hips and face get wider.
- ❀ Your nipples and breasts start to swell.
- ❀ You put on weight and your body shape changes.
- ❀ You might not notice it, but your voice gets a bit deeper.
- ❀ The hair on your arms and legs gets darker.
- ❀ Pubic hair starts growing.
- ❀ Hair grows in your armpits.
- ❀ You might find stray hairs growing in other places, too, like on your stomach, face, or around your nipples.
- ❀ Your skin gets oilier and you sweat more.
- ❀ The hair on your head gets greasy more quickly.
- ❀ You might get spots on your face and body.
- ❀ Your sex organs start to develop — see page 15.
- ❀ Your periods start.

WHAT ABOUT BOYS?

✦✧✦✧✦✧✦✧✦✧✦✧✦✧

I know we girls like to think we're special (and of course we are), but boys go through puberty too, and a lot of their changes are pretty much the same as ours (except for the ones that are totally different, of course...).

As you know (because you're *really smart*, and you've read page 10) most boys start puberty a year or two after girls of the same age. So although men often end up **taller** than women, there are a few years, at around 11 and 12, when many girls can often **tower** over the boys in their class and they tend to be stronger than them, too.

Enjoy it while it lasts, because in a couple of years the boys will have caught up and then it's the other way round. And boys usually go on growing for longer than girls. Most girls reach their full height by the age of 16 or 17, but boys will often **keep on growing** until they are 19 or 20. Once they start, boys also tend to grow more quickly than girls, which is why adult men are generally taller than adult women. At the same time, boys also start developing more strength and weight in their muscles, so that many boys end up being stronger than most girls, too.

BOYS ARE JUST THE SAME...

Like girls, boys get taller, their arms and legs get longer, hands and feet get bigger, and they put on weight. Their shape changes too. Their face grows longer and their shoulders and chest get **wider**. They get hairier on their arms and legs, grow pubic hair and get hairy armpits, but boys also grow hair on their chin and on their chest – which mostly girls don't do.

Like us, their bodies get sweatier and their skin oilier and they can have just as much trouble with spots as we do.

...BUT DIFFERENT

What boys don't do, of course, is they don't grow breasts. They think! But here's a bit of inside gossip – during puberty some boys find that the area around their nipples does swell up and can feel a bit sore. For a boy, **THIS IS A NIGHTMARE!** He's turning into a *girl!* He's not, of course, it's just those hormones getting confused, and eventually the swelling and soreness goes away.

Boys don't get periods either of course. But they don't have a completely easy ride. One obvious and embarrassing change for boys is when their voice 'breaks' and starts to wobble. One minute they're talking normally and the next, they're squeaking like a mouse or **booming** from the bottom of a deep pit.

It only lasts for a month or two, then it sorts itself out and their voice is deeper than it was before. What it means, however, is that their sex organs – their testicles (balls) and penis (willy) – have started to grow and develop, and for boys this is as major an event as starting periods is for girls.

...AND THIS ALL HAPPENS BECAUSE?

You might think that going through puberty is all about growing up, so that you can wear what you want, do what you want, go off to work or university, get your own car and a flat, travel the world and all those things.

And it is, in a way. But as far as your body is concerned puberty is about just one thing – making sure that your sex organs are grown up enough to make babies!

WHAT? How does that work?

The usual way to make a baby is by a man and woman having sex, or what your biology teacher would call sexual intercourse. This is when a man puts his penis inside a woman's vagina and squirts a milky liquid inside her. This liquid is called semen and it contains millions of tiny cells called sperm.

Check out the diagram opposite. The sperm whoosh up the woman's vagina into her uterus (womb) and then into the Fallopian tubes at the top of the uterus. If they meet up with one of the woman's egg cells there they will try to join up with it. If one sperm gets inside the egg then the egg is fertilized, and between them the two cells can start to grow into a baby.

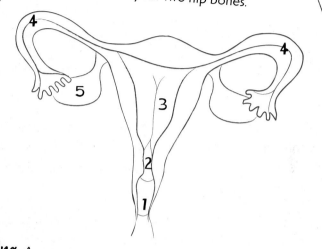

Your internal sex organs
are below your tummy button and
between your two hip bones.

1 Vagina A stretchy tube that leads from an opening between your legs to your uterus. The opening is in the middle, immediately behind the one you pee through (urethra) and well in front of the one that you poo through (anus).

2 Cervix A passage between the vagina and the uterus.

3 Uterus (womb) A stretchy, muscly bag which is where babies grow during pregnancy.

4 Fallopian tube There are two of these tubes, one on each side, leading from the top of the uterus to an ovary.

5 Ovary The two ovaries are like small purses the size of walnuts and contain all the woman's egg cells. A single egg cell is tiny, about half the size of the full stop at the end of this sentence.

MAKING BABIES

Don't worry ... even though puberty is about your sex organs being able to make babies, it doesn't mean that you have to start making them. You still have a lot of other kinds of growing up to do. And then there's all that stuff like getting a job...or going to university...or **travelling the world** that you may want to do one day.

Having sex and making babies is something that most people do when they are fully grown-up and have found someone that they **really love**. Having sexual intercourse is also known as 'making love' and it is one of the things that two people do to show their love for each other – but only when they both feel ready to make love, and when they both want to.

And even then, for many people making love does not always have to mean making a baby. When a couple want to have sex but don't want to have a baby they use a type of *contraception*, like condoms or the contraceptive pill, to stop the egg and sperm from joining up. Making a baby is an incredibly **serious responsibility** and most people only choose to do it when they feel ready and able to take on being a parent and caring for a child.

THE FEEL GOOD FACTOR
You're kidding, right?

If this is all news to you then you might be in a mild state of shock right now, not to mention feeling a bit yucky. Or maybe you've heard bits and pieces about sex before but didn't know whether to believe it.

You are bound to hear other kids your own age or older talking about sex. We all get curious about what sex is at some point in our lives, and that's perfectly okay and absolutely normal. But there are some very confused ideas about sex out there in the world, so don't always believe everything you hear.

The best way to find the answers to your questions is to ask your mum or dad, or another grown-up that you trust and can talk to. If you feel too embarrassed to talk to someone close to you, try asking your favourite teacher, or the school nurse.

Or you could borrow a book about human sex and reproduction (making babies) from a library. Ask the librarian to help you find the right sort of book (it's one of the jobs they love doing). Or you could look on the websites listed at the back of this book for more information.

And if you don't feel ready to find out anything more about it right now, then that's perfectly okay too.

CHAPTER TWO

FROM HIPS TO ZITS

The thing about puberty is that sometimes it can feel like your body has been taken over by aliens from planet Zog! Before it starts you don't think about your body that much, except if you bash your knee or get a cold. But after puberty starts it's like you can hardly stop thinking about it...

☆ ☆ ☆ ☆ ☆ ☆ ☆ ☆ ☆ ☆ ☆ ☆ ☆ ☆

For one thing you wake up one day and find that your clothes don't fit – not even your most *favourite pair of jeans*. Your legs and arms are too long and your hands and feet don't feel like they belong to you any more. You've had a **GROWTH SPURT**.

UPWARDS AND OUTWARDS

When you were younger all the bits of your body grew bigger at the same time. During puberty some bits grow faster than others, and usually it starts with your hands and feet. In fact your feet often grow to their adult size long before the rest of you does.

Your arms and legs get longer next. Then your spine lengthens too, so at least your body looks more in proportion and less like a reflection in one of those **FAIRGROUND MIRRORS** that makes you look like a squashed ball or a beanstalk.

The shape of your face changes, as well. Not as much as for boys, but it does get longer and your cheekbones get wider. And they are not the only things – your hips get wider too and you may get **curvier** around your waist and bottom.

Everyone puts on weight during puberty. Mostly this is down to our **sex hormones** telling our body to store more fat to give it the energy it needs to grow. But because we are all different, some girls seem to get skinnier as they get taller. Usually they are putting on weight as well, but they are growing so fast it is less noticeable.

And while all this is going on you find yourself blundering around like a **ZOMBIE**, tripping over invisible obstacles or even your own feet. Sometimes you feel like the bouncy, active, cheerful girl that you once were has become ... yep, you've got it – **welcome to planet Zog!**

RELAX

IT'S ALL GOOD

You haven't really turned into an alien, but it can take a bit of time getting used to this changing body of yours.

The reason you keep falling over your own feet is because your body is growing so fast that your brain can't keep up. It has trouble working out where your centre of gravity is – so you lose your balance or knock things over. Your brain is really smart, though, so it soon figures everything out and your sense of balance goes back to normal.

Growth spurts don't last forever, either, usually about two or three years. Most girls pretty much reach their full height by the time their periods start and only grow another 5-6 cm after this.

Designer genes

No matter how you may feel about it, how tall you end up being, what size feet you have, or how curvy your hips are – or not – depends on your genes. No, not the jeans you wear, but the genes inside your body. Genes are part of your cells and they control the basic design of your body.

You get a mixture of genes from your parents, who had a mixture of genes from their parents, and so on. So if both your parents are short then it's quite likely that you will be, too. On the other hand, you could end up tall because you have a tall grandmother. It's the same with the colour of your hair and eyes, the type of skin you have, the shape of your face, and so on. It is the way it is and you are who you are.

Of course, that doesn't mean that at some point or other, every one of us hasn't yearned to be taller … shorter … curvier … thinner … with fairer or darker hair … curly haired or straight … blue-eyed or brown. Puberty is a great time for wishing that your body was different in some way. The truth is that there really isn't much you can do to change your basic body design.

But, you can change the way that you think about it...

LOVE

THE SKIN YOU'RE IN
♡ ♡ ♡ ♡ ♡ ♡ ♡ ♡ ♡ ♡ ♡

For a start, try not to compare the way you think your body looks with those of other people – especially all those models and celebrities you see in magazines. They may look very glamorous in photographs, but most of them have to work very hard to look the way they do and they are not necessarily any happier because of it.

It's great that everyone is different. Imagine how weird and boring it would be if we all looked the same, like peas in a pod. There are lots of ways of being beautiful and many of them have less to do with the shape of your body or your face and more to do with the kind of person you are. Someone who is happy, friendly, and interested in other people is much more attractive than someone who is only interested in how she looks.

Remember too that we are all in the same boat. Everyone has bits of their body that they might wish were different – even that girl with the 'perfect' skin and the 'perfect' hair (who is probably so busy worrying about the size of her feet she hasn't even noticed that she has nice hair). The crazy thing is that those bits of our body that we get most worked up about are usually totally invisible to everyone else.

So instead of stressing about the things you don't like about yourself, focus on the ones you do like.

Maybe you have really thick, shiny hair, or a nicely shaped nose, or a great smile, or nice hands.

Learn to accept your body the way that it is. After all, it's going to be with you for a very long time. Think of it as your best friend. It may not be perfect but don't be too hard on it, especially while it still has a lot of growing and changing to do. And while that is happening the best thing you can do for it is to be cheerful and supportive and take care of it.

LOOKING GOOD, FEELING FINE

There's no other way to say this. Your parents are right, and your teachers too. The best way to keep your body healthy and yourself happy is to get enough sleep, get some exercise, and eat properly.

All the growing and changing you do during puberty takes a lot of energy and the only way your body can get that energy is from food. So you really do need to eat three meals a day, especially breakfast, and real food at that – not the junk stuff.

Feeling tired? **Carbohydrates** give you the most energy – foods like bread, pasta, potatoes and rice – and your body needs them. About one-third of all the food you eat in a day should be carbohydrates.

Want healthy hair, nails and skin? That's what **proteins** are for, and they also build and repair body tissue, and help you fight off infections. Eat two portions a day of meat or fish, eggs, beans, or nuts.

Want to be brainier, calmer and overall more brilliant? Then you need some **fats** each day, but the right types of fats. Olive, sunflower and nut oils are good, and oily fish such as tuna and salmon are great.

You need red meat and dairy fats too, just go easy on them. The kinds of fats you find in shop-bought baked goods, biscuits and fried foods are not so good and are best avoided.

What about a perfect smile? You need calcium for gleaming white teeth and strong bones. Make sure you have two or three portions of dairy foods a day, such as milk, yoghurt or cheese.

Want bright sparkly eyes and a healthy glow? Eat as much fruit and veg as you can – at least five portions a day. Include things like citrus fruits (or drink a glass of orange juice), green leafy veg (spinach or broccoli), and tomatoes. Fruit and veg have loads of vitamins and minerals in them, and you need them all to keep your body in great shape. Try to eat as many different colours as you can.

ADDED EXTRAS

Girls need iron (because you lose some each month when you have your period), so learn to love iron-rich foods, like lean red meat, dried fruit, or leafy greens, or foods with iron added to them – like some breakfast cereals.

What we don't need is sugar! Sugar tastes sweet. That's it. That's all it does for you. Sugar is found naturally in many foods, but it's also added to loads of ready-made foods and drinks. Okay, so there are times when only a chocolate bar will do (sigh), but otherwise sugar is best avoided.

RISE AND SHINE

Want to stay up at night, then can't get up in the morning? That's puberty for you. But not getting enough sleep makes every molehill into a mountain. Your body needs to rest in order to grow, so snuggle up with a good book or some soothing sounds and get some early nights.

Being active helps you sleep and is good for you and your body. Lots of girls give up sports once puberty kicks in. They either lose interest, or their body feels uncomfortable. But if running around a hockey pitch isn't your idea of a good time anymore, then try something different.

Dancing is a fantastic way to stay fit. If you don't fancy ballet, try modern dance, jazz, hip-hop, salsa, or even belly dancing! Or how about swimming, or yoga? All these activities will make you feel great, and your body will love you for it.

GIRL TALK WEIGHTY ISSUES

So how often have you heard your mum, older sister, or your brother's girlfriend moan about their weight? Whether they are trying to put it on or take it off, lots of women get hung up on dieting and start trying to live off a lettuce leaf, or 15 boiled eggs a day. But, honestly? Most diets don't work. All they do is make you spend more and more time thinking about your weight.

It's normal to get grumpy about how we look sometimes, but it is not good to become seriously miserable about it – to the point where it's the only thing we can think of. There is really not a lot of use in worrying about your weight during puberty. Your body is doing what it needs to do in order to grow properly, and it is changing so rapidly it's hard to know what kind of shape you will have at the end.

But if you do find yourself getting unhappy because you think you are too fat or too skinny, talk to an adult about it – a parent, teacher, the school nurse or school counsellor. Don't keep it to yourself, or start some kind of 'do-it-yourself' diet. For one thing, you could make yourself really ill if you are not eating properly. For another, your weight is probably not half the problem you think it is, and if you do need to change the way you eat your doctor is the best person to help you do it.

HAIR IN STRANGE PLACES

When you're a child the hair on your body is more or less invisible. But during puberty the hair on your arms and legs becomes thicker and darker. Then one day you discover a few hairs growing around your vagina. **Eeek!** This is pubic hair and it usually looks quite different to the rest of your body hair.

Pubic hair starts off soft and fine but gradually gets darker and curlier. It never grows very long because it is always falling out and being replaced with new hairs. But over a few years it slowly spreads to form a triangle in front of your pubic area and along the tops of your inner thighs. Not long after your pubic hair starts growing you'll probably start getting hairs in your armpits, too.

You might also have a line of dark hairs growing down your tummy, from your navel to your pubic hair. Or you may find a few dark hairs growing around your nipples, or darker hairs on your upper lip. Lots of girls grow hair in all these places. The only major difference is how thickly or how dark the hairs grow, and that's down to those designer genes again.

CHAT ROOM
DO YOU, DON'T YOU?

Having hair on your body is 100% natural for men and women, but some girls panic at the first sight of a sprinkling of stray hairs while others are proud of these signs of womanhood. Whichever way you feel, don't think that you have to immediately rush off and do something about it.

Some women think that body hair looks untidy and unattractive — at least, that's the view that is usually given out by magazines and beauty adverts. Other women think it is more natural and healthy looking, and they don't like the way fashion tries to pretend that women's bodies aren't hairy.

Give yourself time to decide how YOU feel about your body hair. In any case, it's best to let it grow naturally to begin with. Later on, if you do decide you want to get rid of some of it there are various ways of doing it (see next page), but talk to your mum, older sister or friend first.

HAIR TODAY, GONE TOMORROW

There are lots of ways of removing hair from your body. Depending on where the hair is, some are better than others so it's always a good idea to get some advice before you start. These are the ones most people use.

SHAVING

🙂 **Simple to do at home, doesn't cost much, (should be) painless.**

🙁 **Doesn't last long (a few days), grows back as stubble, can cause cuts, skin irritation, ingrown hairs.**

Shaving is fine for legs and armpits. Be careful though, it's easy to cut yourself, so have someone there to help you the first time you do it.

The razor should be clean and sharp – blunt razors can make your skin sore. Make sure your legs and armpits are clean, too.

It's good to give your legs a rub with a bath scrub or brush to remove dead skin cells first. This helps prevent ingrown hairs

— which is when a hair grows back under the skin and causes a small bump that can get infected.

Use warm water and shower gel (or shampoo works just as well) to get your legs good and soapy. Slide the razor up your leg in smooth strokes, starting from the ankle. Don't press hard on the razor, and rinse the soap and hair off it as you go.

Do the same with your underarms, using a downwards stroke rather than side to side. Put moisturiser on your legs and armpits after shaving, but don't use a deodorant straight away, as it will sting like crazy.

If you're not about to go on a beach in your bikini don't bother with the pubic hair at the top of your legs. It's a tricky area to get at and you are more likely to get ingrown hairs or irritation when the hair grows back.

LISTEN UP!

Don't shave other parts of your body, like your face, forearms or stomach. The hair grows back quickly, is stubbly, and you could end up with a rash. In fact, it's best not to remove hair from your forearms at all unless it really, really bothers you. If it does, you could try hair removal cream or waxing, or bleaching, but talk to your mum or another adult you can trust first.

CREAMS

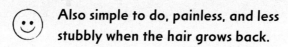

🙂 Also simple to do, painless, and less stubbly when the hair grows back.

🙁 Can irritate the skin, works best on fine hairs, bit messy, smells nasty.

Hair-removal creams work best on smaller areas of skin such as your upper lip or your stomach, but you should do a test patch first to make sure it won't irritate your skin or give you a rash. They are fairly easy to use. Make sure the skin is clean and dry, then spread a thin layer over the hair and wait a while. Chemicals in the cream dissolve the hairs and you rinse the cream off in lukewarm water and dry your skin. Avoid putting make-up or moisturiser on for a while afterwards.

WAXING

🙂 Silky smooth result, lasts for 2-3 weeks, soft re-growth.

🙁 It's painful, it's expensive, can cause skin irritation and ingrown hairs.

Ouch! Waxing can remove all types of body hair, from your face to your legs, but it is a bit painful. It's usually done by spreading a layer of soft wax on the skin and then ripping the wax off with a strip of material. Think pulling off a plaster! The wax glues itself to the hairs so they are pulled out at the roots.

You can buy do-it-yourself wax kits but it really is best to have it done professionally at a beauty salon — which is why it's expensive. If you want to try it, get the bottom half of your legs done first so you can see what it feels like before you move on to more sensitive spots!

PLUCKING

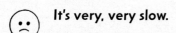

😊 **Cheap, easy, lasts for 2-3 weeks.**

☹️ **It's very, very slow.**

Plucking hairs out with tweezers is brilliant for small areas and the odd bit of facial hair, but it would take you all day to do a leg or an underarm, not to mention making you cross-eyed.

BLEACHING

😊 **Easy to do, cheap, painless.**

☹️ **Works best on small areas and fair skin, can irritate the skin.**

You need a face and body bleaching cream, not the stuff hairdressers use to dye hair. Bleaching is mostly used to lighten facial hairs, but it does also work on larger areas like forearms. Because it doesn't remove the hair there is less problem with re-growth although the bleach itself grows out after a few weeks. Obviously, bleached hairs can still be seen, especially against darker or tanned skin.

DON'T SWEAT IT!

Along with hair, your skin is also covered in tiny holes called pores. These let your body sweat when you get too hot. Normally sweat isn't particularly smelly, but during puberty your body starts making another kind of sweat as well.

This sweat is made in your follicles (little pits holding the root of the hair), but only in some parts of your body – your armpits, pubic area, belly button and, a bit weirdly, your ears. The sweat produced in these areas is a thicker, waxier liquid and it has nothing to do with cooling your body down. We make this kind of sweat when we get nervous or excited.

The problem is, when this sweat mixes with bacteria on your skin it starts to whiff and if you wear tight-fitting clothes made from man-made materials like nylon the smell can start to linger.... **Believe it or not,** some scientists think this smelly sweat is to make us more attractive to the opposite sex. Go figure! But if you're not keen to try out this theory, the answer is pretty simple. Regular washing does the trick.

WASHING UP

Wash your body from top to bottom once a day, especially your face, armpits, pubic area, bottom and feet. And while we're on the subject of washing, girls, remember to always wash and wipe from front to back – that is, from your vagina to your anus – never the other way around. Then you won't run the risk of getting infectious germs into your vagina.

Wear clean underwear, socks or tights every day, and change your other clothes as soon as they start to smell sweaty.

It's fine to wear a deodorant or anti-perspirant if you want to, but don't use them instead of washing and never put them on or around your vagina. Deodorants work on the smelly bacteria, and anti-perspirants make you sweat less. They are sold as sprays or roll-ons. Both work the same but roll-ons are better for the environment.

Don't go crazy, using them once a day is plenty, and try a test patch first, because you could be allergic to them. (In fact, some people think that the chemicals in deodorants could even be harmful to our health.) Remember, there's really no need to wear them at all. If you wash yourself well every day you'll smell great.

SPOT THE SPOT

Spots always turn up when you least want them. Puberty is prime time for pimples and almost everyone gets them.

Hair follicles contain tiny oil-producing glands. The oil protects your skin and hair, and keeps it soft and waterproof. But during puberty oil-production goes into overdrive. The hair on your head gets greasier, and when too much oil builds up on your skin it can block follicles, trap bacteria, and…you have a spot.

Spots can pop up anywhere but mostly you get them on your face, neck, back or chest. They come in lots of varieties, too – whiteheads, blackheads, pimples, and huge red throbbing ones! You might have just one or lots. If you have lots it's called acne.

FACT OR MYTH?

'Chips and chocolate give you spots.'

MYTH!

Spots come from the oil in your skin, not the oils that you eat. How many spots you get mostly depends on the type of skin you have. It's those genes, again. You can also get more spotty just before a period (hormones), and if you get nervous or stressy (so keep calm).

THE FEEL GOOD FACTOR

Help! What steps can I take to zap my zits?

Keep your skin clean. It helps knock back the oil level. Use warm water and a gentle soap or cleanser twice a day, and pat dry with a clean towel. Don't scrub hard, or wash too often, as you'll irritate the skin and take away too many of its natural oils. Don't forget that your skin needs some natural oils to protect it and keep it soft.

Keep your hands clean and away from your spots. NO squeezing! It's really tempting to squeeze them but it will make them worse and you could be left with scars.

Use a non-oily moisturiser and try to resist covering your spots with make-up. It doesn't hide them and it just clogs your skin up even more. Many make-up products can also irritate the skin.

The good news is that acne usually clears up once you've gone through puberty, but if you really can't stand your spots one second longer try some of the many creams and lotions you'll find in the chemist. If they don't work see your doctor. There are medicines that can help.

CHAPTER THREE

THE NEWS ON BOOBS

Can't wait for your boobs to grow, or can't bear the thought of it? Or maybe you're somewhere in-between? However you feel you're not alone. Most of us have a bit of a love-hate thing going on with our breasts. Probably because people make such a big deal out of them and it's like carrying a huge flashing sign on your chest that says: 'I'M A WOMAN!'

☆✨✳☆✴☆✳✳✴☆✳☆✳✳✳☆✴☆

If you're not quite ready for them, growing breasts can make you feel **embarrassed** and *self-conscious*. On the other hand, if all your friends have them and you haven't you could be thinking that you will be **THE ONLY GIRL IN THE WORLD** to never have any. But like all things to do with puberty they will grow when they are ready and not before — and whether it's early or late it has nothing to do with how **big** or **small** they will be.

Breasts usually develop slowly. They begin with a small swelling under the nipple that gradually grows into a bump. The area around the nipple may get larger and darker, and sometimes they can feel a bit **achy** or **sensitive**. At first they tend to look cone-shaped, but after a while they fill out and get rounder. Roughly by the age of 18, most girls' breasts have finished growing.

While they are growing you might find that one breast is sometimes bigger than the other. That's okay, it's nothing to get into a sweat about. They will even up in the end (although no two breasts are ever exactly the same).

GIRL TALK SIZE
DOESN'T MATTER

Girls with small breasts may worry that they are not a 'proper woman', while girls with large breasts can feel as if their boobs are the only things anyone ever sees about them. But there really is no such thing as the 'right' size or shape, everyone is different. Try to accept your breasts as another unique part of you. After all, breasts are there to make milk for your baby if you have one, and size has nothing to do with that.

WHAT ABOUT BRAS?

Okay, so your breasts have started to grow and you need to buy your first bra … or do you? When should you start wearing a bra?

The answer is that there is no 'should' or 'shouldn't' about it. The best time to get a bra is when you feel you want or need one.

There's no law that says you ever have to wear a bra if you don't want to, although as your boobs get bigger you may find that they start feeling a bit wobbly and uncomfortable without any support at all. Especially when you are leaping about on a dance floor or a sports field. And then there's the whole 'nipple pointing through the t-shirt' thing — which can make you feel like the whole world is suddenly staring at your chest!

But even when you do start wearing a bra it doesn't mean you have to stay in one forever. Lots of women sometimes wear them and sometimes don't.

BRA-DI-DAH!

And buying a bra is not that easy. From crop-tops and t-shirt bras to push-ups, cross-overs, underwired, backless and balconies — where do you start?

Trainer bras are brilliant first bras because they are soft and stretchy, don't have lots of seams, padding, or wires around the cups, and don't cost a fortune.

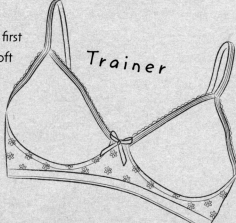

Trainer

But trainer bras don't have a lot of support, either, so when you are doing anything sporty or active you'll need a sports bra. It stops everything flopping about, lets you move your arms around without it sliding half-way up your neck, and helps protect the soft tissue around your breasts.

If your breasts are just beginning and you are feeling a bit left out because all your friends are way ahead of you, then you might want a bra that has moulded or padded cups. T-shirt bras have smooth, seamless cups that won't show up under a t-shirt or other clingy top.

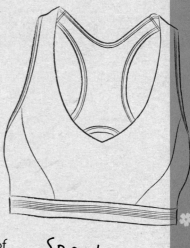

Sports

T-shirt

Or if your breasts feel a bit heavy, try an underwired bra. These have a strip of plastic-covered wire sewn into the seam around the bottom and sides of the bra cup. Some girls love them because they lift and support their breasts, others hate them because the wires can dig in and feel uncomfortable after a while.

Underwired

WHAT'S YOUR CUP SIZE?

No matter what type of bra you choose, it's important to find one that fits properly. And for that you need to know your size.

If you've looked at bras in shops you'll know that they have this weird code on them – 34A, or 38DD. The numbers give you the chest-band measurement, and the letters are the cup size. It works like this:

Loop a soft tape measure right around your chest so that it sits just under your breasts. It's best to do this with nothing on, or just a thin cami vest. The tape measure should not be too tight, but it shouldn't slip. In the UK, bras are measured in inches so you need to know your chest measurement in inches.

If it's an even number add 4, if it's an odd number add 5 (if it's half-way between two numbers take the highest), e.g.

Your chest is 24 inches + 4 = 28 bra band

Your chest is 31 inches + 5 = 36 bra band

Next measure around your chest again, but this time hold the tape higher up across the fullest part of your breast. Keep the tape level and don't squash your breasts. Take this measurement away from your band measurement and the difference is your cup size, so:

Same size or less = AA cup

1 inch difference = A cup

2 inch difference = B cup

and so on…

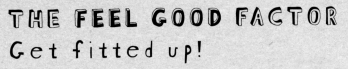

THE FEEL GOOD FACTOR
Get fitted up!

Measuring yourself gives you some idea of your size but it's a tricky business because cup sizes can be different for different band widths and styles. The best thing is to go to the bra department in a big store and ask to be measured.

Before you shriek and curl up in embarrassment, remember that sales people in bra departments are trained to do this and have seen every kind of breast you can imagine. Take your mum, older sister, or friend with you and choose an older sales lady if it makes you more comfortable. She can also give you advice on the different types of bra. Then go wild and try on everything they've got!

But, before you buy that lovely purple spotty bra, stop and think about what you'll be wearing it with. Strong colours and patterns will show through lots of clothes. It might sound a bit boring but it's best to stick to a white or light-coloured bra to begin with. That way it will always go with whatever you choose to wear.

While your breasts are still growing get yourself re-measured every now and then — and later on, too, because they will change in size a bit as your weight changes.

PERIODS, PADS AND PMS

No matter how you look at it, starting your periods is a big event! Not that every woman in the world feels utterly overjoyed about it. No matter how much you might know about having periods, until it happens it still sounds a bit yucky and, well – embarrassing.

☆✶.✦☆✶✦✶✦✶✦✶✦.✦✶✦☆✦☆

Mind you, a lot depends on when you start. If you're the first one in your group you might feel **proud** to have started even if you are **a bit worried** about how you'll cope with them. If you're the last, you might have got pretty fed up of waiting for them by now.

WHAT ARE PERIODS?

A period is when blood comes out of your vagina. That might sound scary because we don't usually bleed unless we've hurt ourselves, but in this case it's totally *normal* and *healthy*.

It lasts for a few days (anything from 3 to 8) and it happens because your sex organs – your uterus and ovaries and all those other bits we looked at on page 15 – have developed enough to start working.

It goes like this:

Once a month one of your egg cells leaves an ovary and heads for the nearest Fallopian tube on its way to your uterus (womb). While it is doing that the uterus starts growing an extra, cushiony lining on the inside, ready to catch the egg when it gets there. This soft, extra lining helps to protect the egg while it is growing into a baby.

But the uterus will **ONLY** catch the egg if it has joined up with a sperm along the way (it's all on page 14). An egg which hasn't been fertilized starts to break up when it reaches the womb, and because the lining isn't needed it falls away as well. Then the unfertilized egg, bits of lining and some blood all leak away out of your vagina – and that's your period.

BUT WHEN WILL I START?

It is truly irritating, but it's just not possible to say for sure. Lots of girls start between the ages of 11 and 14, but some start at 8 or 9, and others don't start until 16 or 17. It depends entirely on your body and your hormones. If your periods are late showing up, *stay cool* and try not to get worked up about it. If it really bothers you check it out with your doctor.

FACT OR MYTH?

'Once you've started periods you have them all your life.'

MYTH!

You stop having periods while you are pregnant. In fact it's often one of the first signs that you are pregnant. Then you start having them again at some point after the baby is born. Most women also stop having periods during their forties or fifties. Gradually they release fewer and fewer eggs and so have fewer and fewer periods until they stop altogether. This is called the menopause.

46

GIRL TALK BY THE WAY...

A healthy vaginal discharge does not smell bad and is not strongly coloured. If you ever notice that your discharge is thicker, smelly, unusually coloured or your vagina is itchy you may have a mild infection. It's nothing to freak out about but you do need to see your doctor and get it treated.

There are some clues you can look out for that tell you your body is getting ready to have periods. Generally, periods don't start until a few years after your breasts have begun to grow. And having pubic hair often happens a year or two before your periods begin. You could also ask your mum when she started. It's fairly likely that you will start your periods within a year or so of the time she started hers.

A dead giveaway is when you notice white or creamy-coloured stains on the inside of your pants. Sounds a bit gross but it's nothing to worry about. It's called a vaginal discharge and it happens when the walls of your vagina start producing a fluid to keep them healthy. But it's also a sign that your periods could start in the next few months. (If you worry about staining your knickers, use a pantyliner – see page 51.)

One day, quite probably when you are least expecting it, you'll go to the loo and see some red or brownish smears in your knickers, or when you wipe yourself there might be some blood on the toilet paper.

This is it! Your period!

The thing to do is **not to panic**. Even if you aren't at home and you haven't got a sanitary pad with you there is always a way around it. So relax, pat yourself on the back — and feel proud that you are part of an exclusive club that only women belong to! And now read on, so you will know just what to do...

YOUR PERIOD

You might have a light period with very little blood, or a heavier one with what feels like buckets of the stuff. But even though it can look like a lot, women normally lose less than half a cup of actual blood during a whole period. Sometimes you might see some blobby bits in with the blood. It sounds totally gross, but it's okay and nothing to worry about — it's only little bits of your womb lining that you lose and renew each month.

Usually, periods happen about once a month, but that could mean anything from about every 25 days to every 32 days. At first your periods will probably be all over the place! You might have one and then nothing for a month or two. Or you could have two periods in one month. They might be light, then heavy, then light again — or the other way round. There's no way of knowing.

Things should settle down after the first year or so, and then you will have a better idea of when to expect your period — see page 56. But in the meantime, *just be super-cool and make sure you are ready for anything!*

GIRL TALK
YOU CAN DO IT!

Some people have weird ideas about periods and it's easy to get confused by things you hear or read. But honestly, even though having a period can be a bit of a hassle sometimes, it really doesn't mean that you can't do most of the things you normally do.

Okay, so you might not feel on top of the world for a day or two and you might get stomach cramps, a headache or your limbs might feel a bit achy, but there are ways of sorting that out – see page 58. And when you don't have cramps there's no reason at all not to go skateboarding, climb trees, run a marathon – or do whatever you fancy. In fact, exercise is good because it can help keep the cramps away.

Taking baths or showers during your period is fine too, and is especially necessary as your hormone level is high so your skin and hair may be extra oily. Even swimming is fine while you are on your period, although you do need to wear a tampon – see page 52 for more on this.

And last but not least, no one can tell when you are having a period. You do not smell strange, or look strange, and as long as you are wearing the right pads or tampons, and you change them frequently, you won't leak through onto your clothes. Now read on...

TOWELS, TAPES AND

You probably know that you need to wear some kind of protection to soak up the blood when you are having a period, and if you've ever looked at the piles of boxes on supermarket shelves you might be surprised at just how much there is to choose from. But mostly it comes down to a decision between **pads** or **tampons**.

It is totally your choice, but it's often best to start with pads (also called sanitary towels) because they are dead simple to use. Pads are thick pieces of padded tissue that sit inside the crotch of your pants. They usually have a waterproof layer on the bottom with a strip of sticky tape to hold them in place on your pants. Some also have sticky flaps, called wings, that fold under the leg holes of your pants. Look for the type that come individually wrapped in small neat parcels so you can always carry some in a pocket, backpack or purse.

HEAVY OR LIGHT?

Pads come in different sizes and thicknesses depending on how heavy or light your period is. This can change during your period – it'll often start off quite heavy but get lighter towards the end. It's also good to wear a heavier pad at night (you'll need to keep your pants on at night, too).

You'll have to experiment a bit, but check the blurb on the box before you buy. It will usually show how absorbent they are – such as 2 drops for light, 3 for normal, 4 for heavy, or similar.

For really light days try a pantyliner instead – this is a smaller, thinner type of pad that's also good for the days when you have a vaginal discharge – see page 47.

Pads should be changed every 3 or 4 hours during the day, even if they aren't heavily used. Otherwise bacteria build up on them and they get a bit smelly, or they could leak.

Wash your hands first, then remove the wrapper and the backing from the sticky tape. Centre the pad along the inside of your pants (between the leg holes) and if the pad has wings fold them down and under the leg holes.

To change your pad, peel it away from your pants, roll it up and wrap it in toilet paper or the original wrapper and chuck it in a rubbish bin. Don't put any kind of pad down the toilet – if it doesn't block the toilet it'll clog up the sewage system and either way it's gross and bad for the planet!

🙂 **Simple and quick; comfy to wear; easy to tell if it needs changing; doesn't show under your clothes.**

🙁 **Can't wear with swimwear, and definitely not when you are swimming.**

TAMPONS,
TUBES AND STRINGS

Tampons are made of the same stuff as pads but squashed down to about the size of your thumb. This is so they can be pushed up into your vagina to soak up the blood there. Sounds icky? Well, it's not that bad, but it does take a bit of practice.

Like pads, tampons come in different thicknesses and are usually individually wrapped. Some are inside a throwaway plastic or cardboard tube to help you insert them. Others are just pushed in with your finger. All tampons have a string at one end. This hangs down outside your vagina so you can pull the tampon out when it is finished with.

TRYING IT OUT

Any girl who is having a period can wear a tampon no matter what age you are. It doesn't hurt when you put one in, especially if you take it nice and slow to start with, but just about everyone is nervous the first time they do it.

Get the smallest size and choose a time at home when you can take over the loo without your dad or kid sister yelling at you. Start by reading the leaflet that comes in the box — it'll tell you exactly what to do. Wash your hands (before and after), and feel around for the entrance to your vagina — so you know where you are going.

Take off the outer wrapping (but NOT the cardboard or plastic tube if that's the type you are using). Take a few deep breaths and try to relax. Remember that the sides of your vagina are VERY stretchy. Whichever type you are using, angle it a little towards your back when you slide it in rather than pushing straight up. Put it in as far as it will comfortably go and make sure that the string is still hanging down outside.

Believe it or not, when tampons are inside you they are so comfortable you can forget they are there, but it is INCREDIBLY important to remember to change them every 3 or 4 hours – even when your period is not very heavy – see why on page 54. To take one out just pull gently on the string. Used tampons should be treated like pads – wrapped in loo paper and put in a bin as it's much better for the environment than flushing them.

☺ **Small and easy to carry around; pretty much invisible to wear, BEST of all you can swim with them in and wear a bikini.**

☹ **Tricky to use at first; can't see if they need changing.**

CHAT ROOM
THE TRUTH
ABOUT TAMPONS

Lots of girls worry about wearing tampons, and you absolutely don't have to use them if you don't want to — pads are completely fine. But there are times when tampons are a handy option so it's worth giving them a go. No matter how you feel about them, though, there are a few things every girl should know.

You won't damage your vagina by putting a tampon inside it and you can't push it past your vagina. You can't lose it inside you, either. There is absolutely nowhere else for it to go. But you can sometimes forget about it, which is not great — see below.

It's almost impossible for the string to break, although it can get tucked up inside your vagina so you have to fish around for it to pull the tampon out. If you can't find the string you can usually grab hold of the tampon itself. And if you can't do either of these things you will have to see a doctor or nurse to get it taken out — as soon as possible.

It is really, really important not to leave a tampon in for more than 8 hours as there's a slight chance you could develop Toxic Shock Syndrome. Read on...

TOXIC SHOCK SYNDROME (TSS)

This is a very rare but serious infection caused by bacteria getting into your bloodstream. Anyone can get it, but leaving a tampon in for too long can increase your chances. The symptoms of TSS when you are wearing a tampon are fever, dizziness, headache, vomiting, diarrhoea, fainting and a blotchy rash. Take out the tampon straight away and see a doctor fast.

The way to make certain you don't get TSS is to always change your tampon every 3 or 4 hours and to use a pad instead of a tampon at least once in 24 hours. The best time is during the night, as then you don't have to change your tampon in the night if you sleep for more than 8 hours. And don't use a thicker size of tampon than you need, especially if you think this means you won't have to change it so often – it DOESN'T! Otherwise, tampons are a doddle once you've got the hang of putting them in.

AND when you are really comfortable using tampons… there is also an alternative out there that is just as invisible, but it's re-usable, safe, cheaper and eco-friendly. It's called a menstrual cup. This is a soft, rubbery cup about 5cm long. You fold up the wide end and push it inside your vagina. Inside, the wide end unfolds to fit snugly against the walls of your vagina so that all the blood runs into the cup. Just take it out and rinse it every 8 hours or less and then put it back in. It doesn't leak or smell, you can sleep and swim with it in, and you don't have to carry tampons or pads around with you. Check out the Mooncup website for more information (see page 91).

KEEPING TRACK

Once you've got over the shock of having periods and everything has settled down a bit, start keeping track of when your periods happen and how long they last. That way you'll be able to work out when the next ones are due.

Use a calendar or a diary to mark down the day your period starts. This is Day 1. To begin with, count 28 days ahead and mark Day 29 – this might be Day 1 of your next period. In fact, you might find your periods usually start on Day 25, or Day 30, or that they swing about somewhere in-between, but whatever it is that's your personal monthly cycle.

Some women also make a note of how they feel a day or two before their period starts, as this can give them an early warning, like getting stomach cramps or aching breasts, or feeling very washed out. Or they might make a note of how heavy or light their periods are.

By the way, loads of women invent their own symbols or codes for doing this – makes it easier and more private.

THE FEEL GOOD FACTOR
What if my period starts unexpectedly?

Always carry a spare pad or tampon and carry it in a small make-up bag. But if you don't have any with you, fold up a wad of toilet paper and put it in your pants. This will give you time to ask your friend, teacher or school nurse for a spare pad. Ladies' loos often have machines that sell them, too, so it's worth remembering to keep some small change in the bottom of your bag.

What if I've leaked onto my clothes?

Okay, this is tough, but still not impossible. If the mark isn't massive, and if you can use a sink without your skirt/trousers on, you can rinse the blood out – USING COLD WATER ONLY! Then squeeze the material with paper towels to soak up some of the water, or hold it under the hand dryer.

If that's not possible, tie your jumper, cardi, gym sweatshirt around your waist so it hangs down over the stain (borrow one if you don't have one). Or ask another girl to get your coat for you so you can wear it until you can see your teacher or go home. If you are really worried, it can be useful to wear dark clothes on the first few days of your period.

WHAT A PAIN!

So, that's your periods all sorted. But, hey, wait a minute! What was that about stomach cramps? Yep, 'fraid so, some girls get period cramps, and these can be a bit of a pain…

Just about all women get some kind of reaction to having their period, even if it's only now and then. Usually these happen at the beginning of a period or a day or two before. You might find that your skin gets extra spotty, or your boobs feel a bit sore. Or that you get an achy, draggy feeling low down in your belly. This is period cramps and it's caused by the muscles in your uterus as they tighten and relax.

Cramps can be fairly mild and a bit uncomfortable, or truly horrendous! If you get the mild kind try to keep moving – lots of gentle exercise like walking can really help – and wearing loose clothing is good too.

If the pains are bad try taking a warm bath, or lie down with a hot water bottle on your tummy. If you need to, ask your mum or dad if you can take a general pain reliever. It may sound impossible, but try to relax as much as you can and don't worry — it will stop eventually. If you regularly get bad cramps, though, it's worth seeing your doctor.

STRESSED OUT!

Having a period can also turn you from a perfectly sweet and lovely human being into a howling monster, or a soggy, sobbing heap, or sometimes both! It's called premenstrual syndrome (PMS), or sometimes premenstrual tension (PMT), and it's those hormones, again.

Not every girl gets it, and not every month. But if you find yourself suddenly wanting to:

- *yell at those closest to you for no reason*
- *chuck something at your best mate*
- *storm off into the sunset so you can 'be alone'*

check your calendar. Chances are your period is due.

There is not a lot you can do about PMS/PMT except wait for it to blow over and try to go easy on your family and friends. Have some early nights, because being tired just makes everything more difficult, and take time out to indulge yourself in a few treats. Curl up with a good book or watch your favourite movie. Go window-shopping with your best friend, or run a bubble bath with gorgeous smellies and have a long soak. Make PMT stand for *'pamper me truly'*!

CHAPTER FIVE

ALL CHANGE!

All this stuff about spots, hair, boobs and bras, and – urgh! – periods might be making you want to head for the nearest cave, but it really isn't as terrible as it might sound. Puberty is a fairly big deal, but most of it happens quite slowly, and everyone who's been through it – i.e. every adult – understands that it can be tough at times (even if they don't always seem very sympathetic!).

✫☆⋆☆✫☆✫⋆✫☆✫☆✫⋆✫☆☆

JUST BEING YOU

One of the unexpected things about puberty is the way it can make you feel. One minute you're messing about with your toys, moaning about your mum **making you eat cabbage**, and barely bothering about anything much from one day to the next. And then it's like the world has come crashing through your door.

You become **much more aware** of other people and what they might be thinking or feeling. In fact, mainly you start wondering what they might thinking or feeling about you! Suddenly you find yourself feeling *awkward* or *shy*. And, horror of horrors, you start worrying about whether or not people will think you are doing or saying something stupid!

At the same time, people keep talking about how you are 'growing up' in a way that can make you feel irritated or anxious, and as if you ought to be someone different instead of just the same old you.

Just being you is fine. In fact, being you is great, because there is no one else quite like you anywhere in the world. That doesn't mean you are perfect, because nobody is. But it does mean you should recognise and **value your good bits**, instead of fixating on what you might think are your less-good bits. Whether they are to do with how you look, or how good or bad you might be at doing stuff.

Having all these new thoughts and feelings about yourself and the world can **feel weird** but it is *totally normal*. As your body grows and changes your brain grows and changes too, and this affects how you think and how you react emotionally to things going on in your life.

61

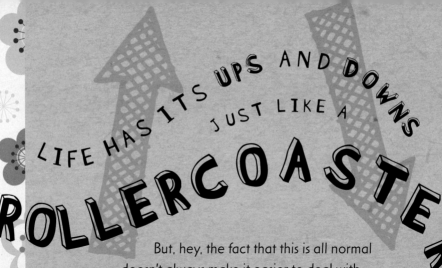

LIFE HAS ITS UPS AND DOWNS JUST LIKE A ROLLERCOASTER

But, hey, the fact that this is all normal doesn't always make it easier to deal with — especially when your emotions are doing a great impersonation of a big dipper! One minute, **everything in your world is rosy** and the next you are totally miserable and you want to scream and shout, or lie on your bed and sob. And the worse thing is you're not sure why!

The 'why' is easy — you're having a mood swing! During puberty your body is loaded up with extra hormones and these upset the balance of chemicals in your brain — which means your emotions swing **wildly** from one extreme to the other.

And if that's not bad enough, your emotions are also way more powerful. So something that mildly annoyed you before puberty will now send you into a towering rage. Or things that made you feel a bit hurt or sad are now the end of the world!

It's horrible when it's happening, and there are times when you might feel like your life is rubbish! Or even, that you are rubbish! But hang on to the fact that it's not and you're not, and that **things really will get easier** once those hormones settle down.

THE FEEL GOOD FACTOR

What can I do when I'm feeling down?

🌸 Take a break and have some 'you' time. Go back to something you used to enjoy doing when you were younger. Growing up is hard work and sometimes you need to remember that it's okay to still be a child.

🌸 Know that you are not alone. Everyone has the same feelings that you do – even those really cool kids who always look like they're on top of everything.

🌸 Talk to your friends. Good friends are great at listening to your woes and helping you feel better about yourself. And you can do the same for them when it's their turn.

🌸 Find an adult to talk to. Try asking your parents or other family members how they felt when they were growing up. They may have some good advice. Or maybe speak to your school counsellor or favourite teacher.

🌸 Let it all out. Keep a diary or write some poems. Draw or paint. Sing, dance or play music. Or if none of these appeal then do something active. However you do it, work off some of that excess emotion.

GIRL TALK O-M-G!

You know how it feels. Your stomach drops to your toes, your throat goes dry, your face is on fire and there's a buzzing in your ears. You are **soooo embarrassed!** And it can happen any time, any where and over any thing – because you are now **totally self-conscious.**

BP (before puberty) it didn't matter too much what clothes you wore or how you did your hair, or that you were the tallest girl in the class. Now, suddenly, it matters **ENORMOUSLY!** That's because you are super-sensitive to how you look and how other people see you – or at least, how you **THINK** they see you.

Being self-conscious is a pain. It gets in the way and stops us doing things we want to do, whether it's wearing something different to everyone else, or trying out for a part in the school play. We tell ourselves we'll look an idiot, or that we won't be as good as all the other smarter, better-looking (or whatever) girls in the room, so best not to try.

Don't give in to it. Everyone has times when they feel **self-conscious** or *embarrassed* and sometimes this is unavoidable. But there are things you can do to help build up your confidence, and the more you do them the easier it gets.

Think about what you want to do and imagine yourself doing it. Look in a mirror and say out loud 'I can do this', then keep on saying it. **Smile**, and feel good about yourself. The physical act of smiling makes us feel happier even if we are not, and having **positive thoughts** about yourself helps drown out those useless nagging negative ones.

Self-confidence is all about how you behave on the outside. You might be wobbling like a jelly inside, but if you stand up straight, look people in the eye, smile and squash down those nerves everyone will think you are oozing with confidence.

And when something embarrassing does happen don't run away and hide, or get angry and defensive. Take a deep breath and just shrug in a 'Hey, it can happen to anyone' kind of way. If people are laughing at you try to smile too, even if you have gone an *interesting shade of beetroot*. If you've made a mistake and messed up it's best to just admit it and say you are sorry. Don't try to hide your mistakes, it'll just make you feel worse.

The less fuss you make about an embarrassing mistake the quicker people are likely to forget it. Because **the big secret** is that most people are too busy worrying about themselves and their own mistakes to bother much about yours!

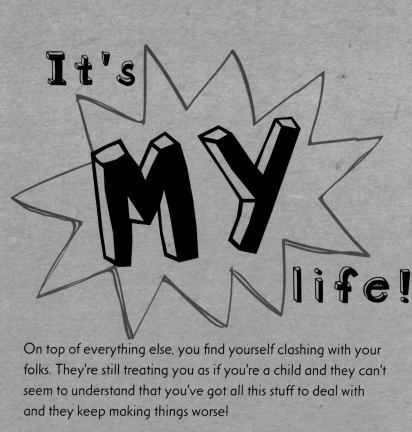

It's MY life!

On top of everything else, you find yourself clashing with your folks. They're still treating you as if you're a child and they can't seem to understand that you've got all this stuff to deal with and they keep making things worse!

Okay, it's time to calm down and get a grip on a few things...

A big part of growing up is wanting to take more control of your life, make your own decisions, and have your opinions listened to. That's fine – up to a point. But there are a few things you have to face up to.

You have to remember that you aren't all grown up yet. You still need your family to care for you and protect you, and no matter how much you argue with them you know you still want their love and support.

FAMILY FEUDS

Puberty can be tough on everyone in the family. Remember that **EMOTIONAL ROLLERCOASTER** you are on? It makes it all too easy for you to shout first and feel sorry later. Having rows with your parents will hurt them as much as it hurts you, so take some deep breaths and try to see their side of things. They've spent years trying to keep you happy and safe. Then you suddenly decide that you know better, that their ideas are old-fashioned, and they should trust you and just let you do things your own way.

But your parents need time to get used to the new you. They can feel just as hurt and rejected by you as you can by them. They can't see inside your head and they won't know what's going on unless you talk to them. So include them in your plans. Negotiate with your parents about your plans and who you intend to go with. Agree a time that you will be home and stick to it. And make sure you let them know as soon as possible if you are going to be late, so that they don't start to worry.

Even if they know you're ready to be more independent they might still worry about whether you will get hurt, get into trouble, or get behind with your schoolwork. They probably know stuff about the world that you don't – and they are just trying to protect you from stuff you haven't encountered yet.

If you want your folks to listen to you, show that you can listen to them. Be willing to meet them halfway and hopefully they will do the same. If there is something you really, really want, you are more likely to convince them if you quietly stick to your guns and keep talking about it – rather than slamming doors and going off in a huff.

RESPECT
IS A TWO-WAY THING!

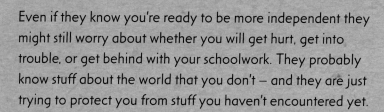

Parents may not be the only people you find yourself falling out with. You might be fighting with your brothers or sisters more than you used to, or you feel that one of your teachers is always getting at you, or the neighbours complain about you playing music too loud – even though it's in your bedroom!

One of the other things about growing up is that as you start wanting people to let you make your own choices and to stop treating you like a child, they start expecting you to be more responsible and to behave more like an adult.

This means remembering that other people have problems, feelings and needs the same as you – and sometimes yours and theirs might collide. It means being aware that the choices you make and the way you behave might make life more difficult for them. It means being polite, recognising that we are all different, and giving other people respect.

This isn't always an easy thing to do, especially if you don't particularly like someone, but if you want people to respect you then you have to be willing to respect them.

TAKING PRIDE IN YOURSELF

It might seem odd, but learning to respect others often starts with respecting yourself. By taking care of yourself and your stuff instead of expecting other people – like your mum – to do it all for you!

Taking care of yourself means eating properly, getting enough sleep, cleaning your teeth and keeping your hair and skin clean. It means looking after your clothes and possessions, and being careful with other people's belongings, too.

But it is also about taking pride in behaving well, such as being on time for things, not telling lies, and doing your best to keep your promises so that people think of you as reliable and trustworthy. And it means recognising what your parents, teachers and others have done for you, and giving something back by looking for ways to be helpful.

Don't worry, no one's expecting you to turn into a saint, but if you aim to do even a few of these things you'll be amazed at the difference it'll make to how you feel about yourself and how others feel about you.

CHAPTER SIX

MATES AND DATES

Friends. Wow! What would we do without them?
They make life interesting instead of boring.
They share all our highs and our lows. They
give us confidence to try new things, and
stand up for us when we are having a bad time.
And best of all, they understand!

☆✦⋆☆✦☆✦⋆✦☆✦☆✦⋆✦⋆✦☆✦☆

But, friends can be a problem too. They can let us down, or say hurtful things behind our backs, or make us feel like we don't measure up — or worse, don't belong. It's tough being an outsider, but having friends that make you feel bad about yourself or that you can't rely on can be just as lonely as not having any friends at all.

PEER PRESSURE!

Fitting in and being part of the crowd is so important it's easy to convince yourself that you have to do what everyone else is doing even if you are not really sure that you want to. Sometimes it's just a question of wearing **certain kinds of clothes** or listening to a particular type of **music**. But sometimes it can be more difficult to deal with.

What if your friends get into watching **HORROR MOVIES** and you don't like to admit that they actually scare you and keep you awake at night? Or maybe they think it's **cool to hang out in town** after school and you have to keep lying to your parents so you can hang out too. No matter what it is, if it makes you uncomfortable and unhappy you need to do something about it.

It's hard to separate yourself from your friends, but it is really important to *trust your instincts* and have faith in your own judgement. It's all part of learning to have **confidence** in yourself. Try telling your friends how you feel, and if they really are your friends they will understand. If they don't get it, then maybe it is time to find other people to hang out with.

FALLING OUT

You are changing and so are your friends and it's easy to find yourselves drifting apart, especially if you move to different schools. But sometimes a friendship that you thought was really solid goes bad and you realise that you and your friend are just not getting on anymore.

Maybe you find yourself getting impatient or irritable with her and that makes you feel bad about yourself. Or maybe she demands a lot from you but doesn't give much back, or turns into a **DRAMA QUEEN** if you want to do something she doesn't. It happens. And when it does you have to ask yourself if you or she are willing to change. If not, it's best to let the friendship go, rather than hang on until you make each other really miserable.

FINDING NEW FRIENDS

Making new friends isn't always easy. What do you like doing? Sports, drama, dance, computers, photography, making stuff? Try joining an after-school club or a youth group. There's lots of things happening out there in the world but you need to go and look for them rather than waiting for them to come to you.

The same thing is true when you find yourself in a room full of people you don't know. Check out page 64 again – feeling self-conscious or shy doesn't help much when you want to meet people. Remember that everyone finds it hard to make friends, so smile, stand up tall, pick out a friendly looking face and think of a question you can ask them. And if it doesn't work the first time, keep trying.

10 WAYS TO BE A BEST FRIEND FOREVER (BFF)!

One important thing to remember is that friendships work best when they are equal. That doesn't mean you have to be the same sort of people, you could be totally different. But it does mean that you have the same kind of liking and respect for each other. In other words, to have a BFF you need to be a BFF, and that means:

- Caring about your friends and giving them help and support when they need it.
- Listening to their side of the story before believing what other people tell you they have said or done.
- Being as honest as you can (without being hurtful) and trying to give them good advice.
- Keeping their secrets (unless it's something you think could harm them) and not gossiping about them.
- Not persuading them to do things they are not comfortable with.
- Not being jealous or possessive about them.
- Saying you are sorry when you've messed things up — and forgiving them when they make mistakes.
- Celebrating their strengths and helping them feel good about themselves.
- Having fun together — no matter how daft or childish.

IT MUST BE
LUURVE!

♡ ♡ ♡ ♡ ♡ ♡ ♡ ♡ ♡ ♡ ♡

When you were younger you might have thought that boys were just annoying and loud. Or maybe it didn't matter to you whether your friends were girls or boys, they were just your friends. But then along comes puberty and things start getting complicated. Your girlfriends get *giggly* and when there are boys around, and boys suddenly seem to have lost the ability to talk to you at all, or can only say stupid things.

Then you discover that there's one boy who isn't at all stupid. In fact he's positively *dreamy* and every time you see him you get a billion butterflies in your stomach. You can't stop thinking about him, and everything he says or does is amazing and vitally important. **You have a crush!**

CRUSH COURSE

Having crushes is how we start learning about having romantic and sexual feelings for people. It doesn't much matter who you have a crush on — it could be a boy in school or a friend's older brother. Or a pop star or someone on telly. Or a teacher or family friend. Or you might have a crush on another girl.

But no matter how much you think that you are totally in love, you aren't, you are only practising. Crushes almost never turn into real relationships. Mostly this is because they only exist in your own head – and that is absolutely fine. Crushes mean that we can daydream about having a beautiful, perfect relationship with someone, without ACTUALLY doing it in real life.

Obviously, if you have a crush on an international superstar you are never likely to meet them anyway. And while it's okay to admire an adult or someone a lot older than you, and to think that they are really cool, it's not okay to believe that you could ever have a real live romantic relationship with them.

FACT OR MYTH?

'If you fancy another girl you must be gay.'

MYTH!

Having romantic or sexual fantasies about people of the same sex as you doesn't automatically mean that you are gay or a lesbian. Your emotions are very intense during puberty and it is easy to have strong, even physical feelings for someone you admire or really like. Don't rush to put a label on yourself – or on anyone else. Give yourself time and it will all become clear.

SHOW AND TELL?

But what if your crush is your age, in your school maybe, and therefore possibly within your reach? What then? Do you let him know how you feel? Get your mate to tell him? Stew in silence while someone else whisks him away? But what if you scare him off, or he thinks you are a complete idiot?

Letting someone know that you fancy them can be risky, but if you don't give it a go you will never know what might have been. If they have no idea who you are, try to get to know them a bit before blurting out your undying love. It's always possible you might discover they are not as hot as you thought they were!

Don't spend too much time worrying about what they might or might not think of you — it will just drive you crazy. Instead, find out what they are interested in. It will give you something to talk about and may be a way of spending time together. Try not to be too pushy or to put someone on the spot in front of their friends — or yours. You don't want to make them feel embarrassed.

GIRL TALK CRUSHED!

In spite of the fact that you are totally gorgeous, no matter how hard you try your crush might not be interested. While this can be pretty devastating, don't beat yourself up about it. It does not mean you are ugly or unlovable or any of those things. It just means the chemistry between you isn't right. Nobody knows why we are attracted to some people and not to others – it's one of life's great mysteries. It can be disappointing and make you feel sad, but the sooner you put it behind you the easier it will be. Don't sit at home moping about it, talk it over with your best girlfriend and then go out and have some fun.

Aim to be relaxed and friendly, and maybe suggest doing something simple, like going for a walk, having ice cream or going to watch a movie. (Have another look at the advice on self-confidence on pages 64-5.)

Of course, you don't have to do anything at all about your crush if you don't want to. You might be happy just to enjoy the daydreams without the pressure of putting them to the test. That's absolutely fine, too, especially if your crushes tend to come and go – which they often do.

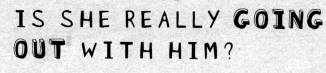

IS SHE REALLY **GOING OUT** WITH HIM?

At some point, someone is going to ask you out for a date.

OMG! What do you do?

If it's someone you know and like, that's great, but remember to check in with your parents, because depending on how old you are they are likely to have some thoughts about what's okay and what's not okay, and it is important they know where you are going and who with.

Even if you really like someone, you could still feel a bit nervous and unsure about spending time with your date on your own. If that's so, why not suggest that you go out with friends that you both know?

remember

Don't feel you have to say yes if you don't want to, or even if you are not sure. It's never a good idea to go on a date just to impress your friends, or because they think you should.

But when you say no, remember to go easy on the person who asked you. No matter how flustered or nervous you may feel, it'll be ten times worse for them. So even if you do think you wouldn't go out with them if they were the last person on Earth, DON'T say so! Remember how you would feel if you were in their shoes and come up with a polite excuse.

THE FEEL GOOD FACTOR
My BFF is so busy with her boyfriend she's got no time for me!

This is a tough one. It is easy to feel hurt and abandoned by your friend, and that can make you feel angry and resentful. But try not to let it show. If you start making demands on her she will start resenting you and then you'll both end up in an argument.

Be patient and remember that her emotions are swamped with excitement over her new relationship. Hang in there and things are bound to calm down eventually. And if she and the guy break up, she will definitely need you to be there.

However, if she and the boyfriend become a regular item you will have to get used to the fact that you will see less of her. Try telling her that you miss her company and the things you used to do together and suggest having a girls-only outing when her boyfriend's not around. You will probably find that she is missing you, too. And whatever happens, don't stay in your bedroom and mope. Get out and start making some new friends yourself!

CHAPTER SEVEN

STAYING SAFE

There are lots of really amazing things about growing up. You can do things and go places you never could as a child. You can choose your own clothes and hairstyles, get yourself to school and back, organise your own social life, and discover all kinds of cool stuff that you wouldn't have been interested in when you were younger.

✦✦✦✦✦✦✦✦✦✦✦✦✦✦✦

But these new freedoms and new abilities also bring new responsibilities and new pressures. Your parents and your teachers expect you to **WORK HARDER** at school and maybe to **help out more** at home. You have to make choices about whether to get your work done or see your friends. Choices about which clothes to buy and whether they will look right. And about **who you hang out with**, and where you go. And then there's all that body stuff going on too.

It can all get a bit much sometimes.

GOOD DAYS, BAD DAYS

There will be some days when nothing seems to go right. When it feels like everyone is getting at you or everything you try to do is a mess. Maybe you feel like you hate everyone and everything, or that you just want to *hide in bed – forever!*

It's okay. Everyone gets days like that. (Remember those mood swings?) Usually these kinds of feelings hang around for a bit and then life moves on and you get over it. But if that doesn't happen, if you feel unhappy, angry or helpless a lot of the time, and if it's **making you feel ill** and like you don't want to do anything or see anyone, then you might be depressed.

Depression is an illness like any other. It doesn't mean you are crazy or useless, or that people will think that you're **WEIRD** – even if you haven't got a clue why you feel this way. But it does mean that you should see your doctor so that he or she can help you to get better. Have a look at page 88 for some advice on getting help.

BULLY BLUES

Sadly, one very common reason for getting depressed is if you are being bullied. Bullying can happen to anyone, at any time of their life. It can happen at home, at school or work, on the street or in a public place, or online.

Being bullied is when the same person or people keep doing or saying horrible things to you. Sometimes bullies say they are just joking, or teasing. But it's only a joke or teasing if the person it is aimed at can see the funny side of it too. If it is hurtful or upsetting it is bullying.

If you are bullied, it is never your fault. You are not the loser — the bully is.

Bullying can happen in all sorts of ways. People might say nasty things about you or your family. They might tell lies about you, or make fun of you in front of others, or try to get your friends to leave you out of things. They might steal from you, or force you to give them your stuff, or physically attack you.

Being bullied can make you feel helpless and as if it is somehow your fault, which is exactly what bullies want you to feel. They know they are doing wrong, which is why they often threaten to make things worse for you if you tell anyone what is happening. But even though it can be the hardest thing in the world – you must tell someone. Bullies have to be stopped, for everyone's sake.

TIPS FOR BULLY BUSTING

If you are bullied at school tell your parents or carers and one of your teachers. Schools usually have a system for dealing with bullying. If you are bullied on the street your parents should report it to the police. If a brother or sister is bullying you at home try to tell a parent. If you can't talk to your parents, maybe there is an aunt, uncle, grandparent or another adult you can talk to. There are also helplines you can phone. You'll find some numbers when you visit the websites listed on pages 90-91.

Tell your friends what is going on so they can help you, too. Bullies usually pick on one person rather than a group. Try to stay out of the way of whoever is bullying you, and if you can't, try not to let them see how angry or miserable you are. Bullies want to see you get upset so if you can pretend that you don't care it is less satisfying for them. It can help to realise that most bullies are actually hugely lacking in self-confidence, but hide their anxiety by being aggressive to other people.

CYBER BULLYING

A cyber bully is someone who sends a nasty text or picture message to your phone, or writes you a vile or hurtful email. If you visit chat rooms or use instant messaging, you might see something rude or repulsive written about you. One of the bad things about cyber bullying is that you often don't know who is sending you these messages. Or worse, they might be pretending to be one of your friends.

But no matter how hurt or angry they make you feel, don't reply to them. As with all bullies, the person who sent it to you wants to get a reaction from you, so if you don't reply they may give up. And, if you blow your top you could be blamed for cyber bullying in turn.

Do keep the messages and show them to an adult you trust – even if it's something really embarrassing or horrible. Cyber bullying can be traced and it is against the law. If you can't tell someone you know, check out the helplines on pages 90-91.

BE CYBER SAVVY

Don't give your mobile number to anyone you haven't actually met, even if they are a 'friend of a friend', or someone you've chatted to online. Remember not to text or send a picture message to anyone you haven't met, either, even if it's an online buddy, as once you do they will have your mobile number. If you get a text or picture message from someone you don't know, don't reply to it but show it to an adult you trust.

Don't open emails sent to you by people you don't know, and never reply to them. They might contain a virus that could attack your computer, or they could be fake messages trying to get information about you, such as your address or phone number, or even just checking that your email address is a real one so they can sell it on to people trying to sell you stuff. Any time you are unsure about an email just delete it or show it to an adult you trust, before you open it.

Be super careful about the information you give out when you are online, in chat rooms or on networking sites. Even chatting generally about where you live or the school you go to can give away more about you than you realise. Use a codename for yourself and – **never tell anyone your real name or your home address** no matter how cool they may seem.

It is easy for people to lie about who they are on the internet – even if they send you a photo you can't be sure it is really them. And definitely don't send someone you haven't met a photo of yourself, or give them access to your profile. Most important of all – **don't ever agree to meet up with anyone you have only chatted to online.** If someone wants to meet you tell a trusted adult straight away.

WHEN YOU ARE
OUT AND
ABOUT

The world is a fun place, and as you get older you will want to go out and do stuff with your friends rather than your parents. That's normal – but part of growing up is also about looking out for your own safety.

- Make sure your parents or carers know where you are going, when you will be back and how you are getting home.

- Don't walk on your own after dark or through parks or waste ground or other out of the way places. Go with a friend to their house and phone your parents for a lift from there.

- If you catch a bus on your own, wait at a busy well-lit bus-stop and sit at the front near the driver.

- Never take lifts from strangers, or stop and talk to a stranger in a car.

- If strangers try to talk to you, even if they are older kids, ignore them and keep walking. Don't accept anything they may try to give you.

- If someone is bothering you, yell at them as loudly as you can to go away, and head for a shop or somewhere where there are other people. NEVER be embarrassed or afraid to ask for help.

GIRL TALK

IF BAD STUFF HAPPENS

Your body is this fabulous, perfect, and totally private thing. If anyone ever tries to touch any part of your body in a way that you don't want them too, that seems weird or unusual, or hurts you, or makes you feel frightened or embarrassed, you are being sexually abused and that person is doing something wrong.

Sexual abuse includes being harassed or teased about your body in a sexual way, or being threatened or pressured into doing something sexual when you don't want to – even if the person involved never actually touches you.

Sexual abuse of any sort is incredibly frightening and harmful – and it is NEVER, EVER your fault. No matter who the abuser is, especially if it is someone you know or even someone you love or have a close relationship with, it is never okay and it should never be kept secret.

No matter how impossible it seems or how scared you are, you must find a way to tell someone about it as soon as you possibly can.

I NEED HELP!
WHAT DO I DO?

When something goes wrong in your life it can make you feel ashamed, **embarrassed**, scared, **ANGRY** or just plain dumb! But it doesn't matter how small or how big your problem is, never be afraid to ask for help. Just talking about it will make you feel a whole lot better, no matter what.

Believe it or not, lots of adults understand how tough things can be and will do their best to help you. Try to pick a time when the person you want to talk to isn't frantically busy. You could tell them you'd like to talk about something and ask them when they will be free. If the first person you try won't listen or doesn't believe you then find someone else. Don't give up!

Parents are the best people to ask, but if you can't talk to anyone in your family, try one of your teachers or the school counsellor or school nurse, or make an appointment to see your family doctor. Doctors can help with all sorts of things and they do not have to tell your parents if you don't want them to – unless this would be harmful to you.

There are also lots of helplines and advice centres you can call. The websites on pages 90-91 are a good place to start, and if they can't help you with your problem they will be able to tell you who can.

THE FEEL GOOD FACTOR
Because you're worth it!

The next few years will bring good days and bad days, and before you know it you will be past them and moving on. Along the way, remember to stand up tall and look the world in the eye. This is your world and you belong here, as does every member of the human race.

Never forget that you are extraordinary. Your body and your brain are perfectly designed to care for you, carry you through life, and enable you to do all sorts of fantastic things — as long as you care for them in return. Be good to yourself. Think about your health and how to take care of your body and mind. Don't be too hard on yourself if things don't go the way you want them to. Learn to trust your instincts and make good choices, and remember to think about others as well as yourself.

You have a lot to look forward to.
Be strong, be positive, be kind —
breathe, relax and enjoy.

GET CONNECTED!

These organisations and websites are specifically for young people. Some also give helpline numbers you can call.

Beat www.b-eat.co.uk
Beat helps young people and adults deal with eating disorders. The website gives loads of information on how to recognise and cope with an eating disorder. There is also a helpline, an email advice service and an online chat forum.

Beatbullying/CyberMentors
https://cybermentors.org.uk
CyberMentors is run by an organisation called BeatBullying (www.beatbullying.org). It's an online chat forum where you can post messages or talk to someone about being bullied, or about anything else that may be making you miserable. Most of the counsellors at CyberMentors are young people themselves who have been trained to give help and advice.

Being Girl www.beinggirl.ie
This website is hosted by the makers of sanitary products but does has lots of useful info and advice about puberty and body issues for girls. There's also an 'Ask Anna' section, plus lots of games and quizzes.

Childline www.childline.org.uk
This website has a free 24-hour phone helpline for young people who have any kind of problem, large or small. If you are not sure about talking directly to a counsellor you can have a private chat online, or send an email through their website.

Get Connected www.getconnected.org.uk
Offers support and advice on finding the right people to help
with your problem. See their website for different ways you can
contact them.

Kidscape www.kidscape.org.uk
This charity focuses on bullying and cyber bullying. It has a
helpline for parents to call if their child is being bullied, but not
for young people to call directly. However, there is information
and advice on the website written for young people.

KidsHealth http://kidshealth.org
KidsHealth is divided into sections for parents, kids, and teens.
Each is packed with info about mind, body, health, fitness, food,
friends and just about any issues you can think of.

Mooncup www.mooncup.co.uk
Check this website for information on what Mooncups are, how
they work and how to use them.

NHS www.nhs.uk/LiveWell/TeenGirls
The part of the National Health Service (NHS) website that
gives specific information on health issues for teens.

Thinkuknow www.thinkuknow.co.uk
Information and advice for young people about abuse of any
sort, including sexual abuse and cyber bullying. There is a link
that allows you to report online abuse, plus films, games and
other information about cool ways to use the internet, how to
stay safe.

USEFUL WORDS

abuse Being frightened, threatened or hurt by someone in any way, whether it is physical, emotional or sexual.

anus The small opening behind your vagina through which you poo.

bacteria Tiny life forms that can only be seen through a microscope. Some are harmful but others help keep us healthy.

cervix A tight, narrow passageway between the vagina and the uterus.

contraception Devices used to prevent a sperm cell from fertilizing an egg cell, such as condoms that catch and contain the sperm, or the contraceptive pill, that work on the egg or the uterus to prevent fertilization.

depression Feeling deeply unhappy for a long period of time. It can lead to a lack of interest in anything, a lack of energy and a sense of hopelessness.

egg cell A female sex cell that carries half of the information needed to make another human being.

Fallopian tubes Part of the female sex organs. Two tubes leading from the ovaries to the uterus. When an egg cell leaves the ovary it travels along the fallopian tube. If sperm are present the egg cell may be fertilized.

fertilized When a female egg cell joins up with a male sperm cell and develops into a baby.

gay Another word for homosexual. A homosexual person is sexually attracted to people of the same sex as themselves. Homosexual women are also called lesbians.

genes Tiny pieces of information that live in your cells. Every human cell carries thousands of genes and each gene describes something about you, such as the colour of your hair, the shape of your hands, or even the way you smile.

growth spurt A time of fast growth during puberty, during which you normally come close to your final adult height.

hormones A group of chemicals that carry messages between cells in the body in order to make them stop or start doing something. They control things like body temperature, growth, our ability to fight off disease and our ability to have children.

lesbian A gay woman.

menopause The time when women gradually stop releasing egg cells and stop having periods. After the menopause women cannot become pregnant.

monthly cycle The number of days from Day 1 of your period until Day 1 of your next period. Generally this is a 28-day cycle, but it can vary from woman to woman and also from period to period.

mood swings Switching from one emotional state to another very quickly and for no particular reason, usually caused by hormones during puberty.

ovaries Part of the female sex organs. There are two ovaries and they contain all of a woman's egg cells. Women are born with all their egg cells already inside them.

penis The part of the male sex organs that puts sperm inside a woman's vagina. A penis is normally soft, but when a man is sexually excited, his penis hardens so that it is able to push inside the vagina. This happens during sexual intercourse.

period Also called menstrual period. This is when blood and an unfertilized egg cell leave the uterus and flow out of the vagina. Each period usually lasts for about 3 to 5 days.

premenstrual tension (PMS) Also called premenstrual tension (PMT). Feeling emotionally sensitive or upset just before or at the beginning of your period.

pubic hair The patch of hair that grows around the external sex organs.

semen The milky liquid that carries the male sperm cells as they travel from the penis into the vagina.

sexual intercourse The usual method by which humans reproduce, when a man puts his penis inside a woman's vagina and releases sperm cells into her body.

sperm cell A male sex cell. Sperm carry one half of all the information needed to make another human being.

testicles Part of the male sex organs. Men have two testicles that hang down on either side of the penis. The testicles make sperm cells and male sex hormones, such as testosterone.

toxic shock syndrome (TSS) A rare but potentially serious bacterial infection that can be caused by wearing the same tampon for too long.

urethra A narrow tube leading from the bladder to an opening through which you pee.

uterus Also known as the womb. Part of the female sex organs. It is where a fertilized egg cell stays and develops into a baby until it is ready to be born.

vagina A muscly tube leading to the uterus.

vaginal discharge A clear or creamy fluid that comes from the vagina and helps to keep it clean and healthy.

93

INDEX

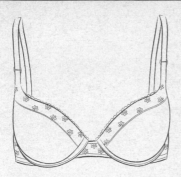

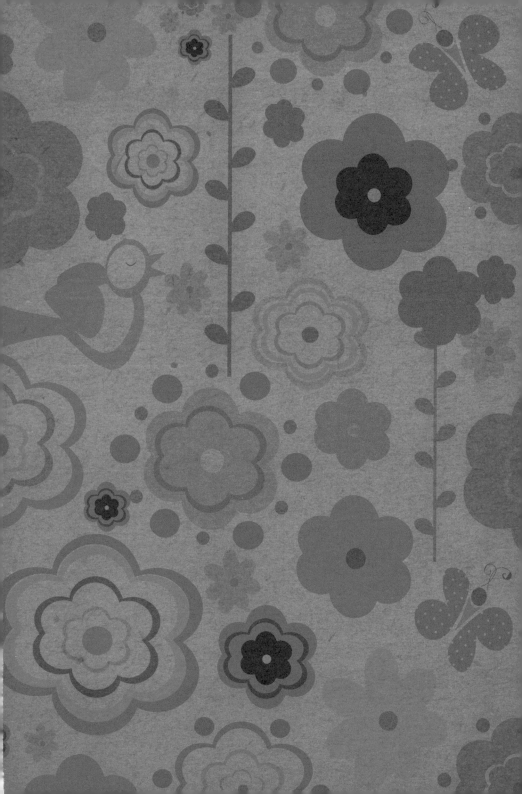

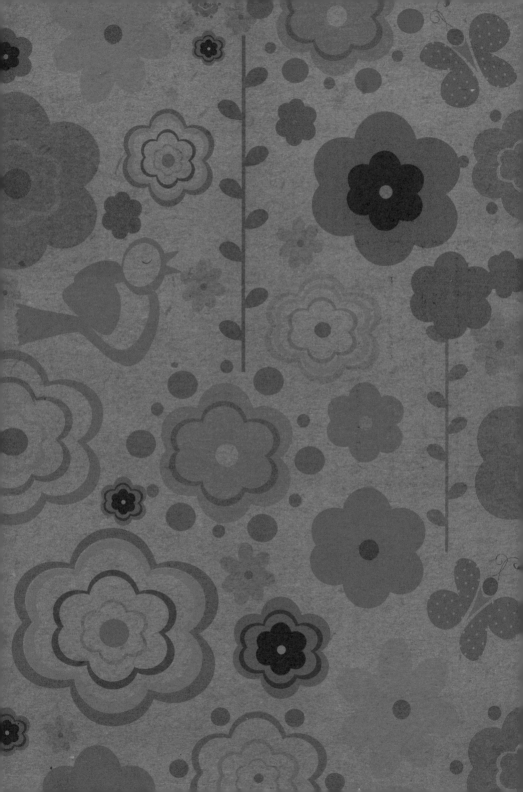